Drinks, Mocktails, and Smoothies for Health and Vitality

Hydrating Recipes for Liver Care and Whole-Body Wellness

Regina Bowman

Table of Contents

Introduction

Welcome to *Drinks, Mocktails, and Smoothies for Health and Vitality: Hydrating Recipes for Liver Care and Whole-Body Wellness*. This book is crafted with a simple, decisive goal: to provide delicious, nourishing drinks that support liver health and enhance whole-body vitality. With an array of smoothies, mocktails, and beverages, these recipes emphasize the importance of hydration, nutrient density, and natural ingredients to aid in liver function and detoxification.

Why Liver Health Matters

The liver is one of the body's primary organs for filtering and detoxifying, playing a crucial role in processing nutrients, metabolizing fats and proteins, and breaking down toxins. Our liver removes waste and converts nutrients from our foods into essential compounds that fuel nearly every bodily function. When the liver functions optimally, it supports better digestion, balanced energy levels, improved metabolism, and even clearer skin and mental clarity.

Supporting liver health with the proper nutrition can help ease its workload, promote natural detoxification, and boost overall vitality. That's where hydrating, nutrient-rich drinks come in.

The Role of Hydration and Nutrient-Rich Drinks in Detox and Wellness

Proper hydration and nutrient-dense beverages can do wonders for liver function and overall health. Staying hydrated is essential because water assists in flushing out toxins, keeps our cells functioning well, and aids the liver in breaking down harmful substances. But it's not just water that matters—adding antioxidants, vitamins, and minerals through nutrient-rich drinks provides the liver with the essential compounds it needs to function effectively.

In this book, you'll find recipes that are designed to nourish, cleanse, and invigorate, using ingredients such as leafy greens, berries, citrus fruits, and superfoods like turmeric, ginger, and spirulina. These ingredients are hydrating and full of liver-supportive nutrients like antioxidants, fiber, and essential vitamins.

Our recipes offer a wide variety of flavors and textures, from fruity, hydrating mocktails to creamy, protein-packed smoothies. Each recipe is a delightful exploration of taste and texture, designed to invigorate your senses and keep you excited about your health journey. Whether you're looking to revitalize your mornings with a nutrient boost, unwind with a liver-friendly mocktail, or simply hydrate with purpose, these recipes are easy to integrate into daily life and are crafted to be as enjoyable as they are beneficial.

Let's embark on this journey toward better health, one drink at a time. With these revitalizing recipes, you are taking an active role in supporting your liver, boosting your hydration, and elevating your wellness, sip by sip. This is your journey, and you are in control.

Chapter 1: Key Ingredients for Liver-Friendly Beverages

In this chapter, we dive into the ingredients that make these liver-friendly beverages genuinely impactful. Below, you'll find a breakdown of the herbs, superfoods, low-sugar fruits, and hydrating ingredients that will bring your drinks to life.

Herbs and Spices for Detoxification

Herbs and spices are often overlooked in beverages, yet they add not only flavor but also powerful detoxifying properties. Here are a few essential herbs and spices featured in these recipes:

Turmeric: Known for its anti-inflammatory and antioxidant properties, turmeric contains curcumin, a compound that protects liver function against cellular damage. It's also excellent for aiding digestion and supporting the body's natural detox pathways.

Ginger: Ginger adds a warm, spicy kick to drinks and is a well-known digestive aid. Its antioxidant properties support liver function by helping to break down toxins more efficiently. Plus, ginger can reduce bloating, making it ideal for post-meal drinks.

Mint: Refreshing and aromatic, mint can aid digestion and soothe the stomach. Mint's natural oils stimulate the production of bile, which aids in digestion and helps the liver eliminate waste products more effectively.

Superfoods for Boosting Health

Superfoods are nutritional powerhouses, often packed with antioxidants, vitamins, and minerals that promote liver health and overall wellness. Here are some top superfoods to include in liver-friendly beverages:

Spirulina: This blue-green algae is rich in protein, iron, and antioxidants, which help support detoxification and reduce oxidative stress. Spirulina is also high in chlorophyll, which can aid in removing heavy metals and other toxins from the body.

Chia Seeds: These tiny seeds are high in omega-3 fatty acids, fiber, and antioxidants. When soaked, they absorb water and create a gel-like texture that adds creaminess to drinks while also helping to slow digestion and regulate blood sugar levels.

Beetroot supports liver function by increasing enzyme activity and bile production, helping the liver to process fats. Rich in nitrates, beets improve circulation, which can also aid in nutrient delivery to the liver.

Leafy greens are rich in chlorophyll, which can help detoxify the liver by neutralizing heavy metals, chemicals, and other toxins. They're also high in fiber and antioxidants, supporting liver function and helping to lower levels of fat in the liver.

Low-Sugar Fruit Choices and Hydrating Ingredients

For liver-friendly beverages, we focus on low-sugar fruits that are packed with antioxidants, fiber, and hydration. These fruits support liver health and keep blood sugar levels stable, promoting sustained energy.

Berries: Blueberries, strawberries, raspberries, and blackberries are excellent low-sugar fruits loaded with antioxidants like anthocyanins, which protect the liver from oxidative damage. Their fiber content aids digestion, further supporting detoxification.

Citrus Fruits: Lemons, limes, and grapefruits are high in vitamin C and compounds that stimulate liver enzymes and support detoxification. They add a bright, refreshing flavor to drinks, helping with bile production.

Kiwi is a nutrient-dense fruit with fiber, vitamins C and E, and antioxidants, all contributing to liver health. It adds a tangy sweetness to beverages, with a relatively low glycemic index, making it ideal for maintaining balanced blood sugar levels.

Cucumber is an incredibly hydrating vegetable due to its high water content. It's a great addition to drinks for added refreshment and is also naturally cooling and soothing for the digestive system.

Coconut Water: Often called "nature's sports drink," coconut water is naturally rich in electrolytes like potassium, magnesium, and calcium. It's low in sugar and provides hydration, making it an ideal base for smoothies and mocktails.

Each of the ingredients has been carefully chosen to provide maximum benefits with minimal impact on blood sugar. In the next chapter, we'll dive into how to use these ingredients to create flavorful, health-boosting drinks that you can enjoy daily to support liver function and overall vitality.

Let's start blending, hydrating, and nourishing from the inside out!

Chapter 2: How to Build a Healthy Drink Routine

Creating a healthy drink routine can transform how you feel, energize your body, and improve your liver health. With some planning, you can easily incorporate hydrating, detoxifying, and nutrient-rich beverages into your daily routine to help support your liver, boost energy, and improve your overall wellness. This chapter explores how hydration impacts health and the best times to enjoy these liver-supporting drinks for maximum benefit.

The Importance of Hydration for Overall Health

Hydration is the foundation of good health. Every cell, tissue, and organ in the body relies on water to function correctly, and hydration is especially crucial for the liver, which needs adequate water to process toxins and support digestion.

- **Promotes Liver Detoxification**: The liver processes toxins and waste, which are then removed from the body via the kidneys and urine. Staying hydrated helps flush out toxins more efficiently, reducing the strain on your liver.
- **Aids Digestion**: Water aids in the digestion and absorption of nutrients, which the liver can then use to support detoxification and other vital functions.
- **Supports Energy Levels**: Dehydration can lead to fatigue and low energy, making it harder for your liver to function optimally. Hydrating drinks can boost both physical and mental energy.

Including liver-friendly beverages such as smoothies, mocktails, and herbal infusions in your daily routine provides additional nutrients and antioxidants to support overall health, reduce inflammation, and promote balanced hydration.

Best Times to Enjoy Detoxifying and Refreshing Beverages

To make the most of your liver-supporting drinks, timing is key. Here are some of the optimal times to enjoy these drinks for maximum benefit:

Morning Hydration Boost: Starting the day with a hydrating, nutrient-rich drink can kick-start your metabolism, support digestion, and prepare your liver for the day. Try beginning your morning with a glass of lemon water, a green smoothie, or a liver-friendly juice to get your hydration off to a strong start.

Mid-Morning Replenishment: A mid-morning beverage, like a smoothie or herbal tea, helps bridge the gap between breakfast and lunch, providing sustained energy and keeping you hydrated.

Pre-Meal Digestive Support: Drinking a small amount of water or a lightly infused herbal drink before meals can help digestion, ensuring the liver is primed to handle incoming nutrients. This can also curb appetite and prevent overeating.

Post-Meal Cleansing Drink: After meals, a gentle detox drink such as a ginger or mint infusion can support digestion, reduce bloating, and encourage liver activity. Avoid heavy or sugary drinks right after meals, as they can interfere with digestion.

Evening Relaxation: Calming herbal teas or low-sugar smoothies with soothing ingredients like turmeric or chamomile can support your body's natural evening detox process. These options promote restful sleep, essential for liver regeneration and cellular repair.

By thoughtfully incorporating these drinks at optimal times, you're setting up a routine that benefits your liver and your entire well-being.

Drink Tips for Optimal Flavor

Creating liver-friendly drinks that taste delicious without relying on excess sugar can be simple and fun. With the right ingredients and techniques, you can make smoothies, juices, and mocktails that balance sweetness naturally while providing targeted health benefits, such as enhanced energy, immunity, and detoxification. This chapter offers practical tips to help you master flavor balancing and how to customize drinks based on your wellness goals.

Balancing Sweetness without Excess Sugar

One of the critical challenges in creating liver-friendly beverages is achieving just the right amount of sweetness without adding excess sugar, which can be hard on the liver. Here are some techniques for enhancing sweetness naturally:

- **Use Naturally Sweet Fruits**: Opt for fruits lower in fructose but high in flavor, such as berries, green apples, or kiwi. Bananas and mangoes are also excellent choices in moderation, as they add both sweetness and a creamy texture to smoothies.
- **Incorporate Flavorful Herbs and Spices**: Adding cinnamon, vanilla, or a pinch of nutmeg can enhance the perception of sweetness without any added sugars. These spices also come with antioxidant properties, which support liver health.
- **Try Low-Sugar Sweeteners**: Small amounts of stevia, monk fruit, or a hint of raw honey (if it fits within your dietary goals) can add sweetness without significantly impacting blood sugar.
- **Balance with Citrus or Green Vegetables**: Including a splash of lemon or lime or adding greens like spinach or cucumber can provide a refreshing contrast that balances sweetness naturally, reducing the need for added sugars.

Customizing Drinks for Energy, Immunity, and Detox

Liver-friendly beverages can also be tailored to meet specific wellness goals by incorporating targeted ingredients known for their health benefits. Here are ways to customize your drinks for energy, immunity, and detoxification:

For Energy: Add ingredients that provide sustained energy without causing spikes in blood sugar.
Try incorporating:

- Leafy greens such as spinach or kale, high in iron and B vitamins, are essential for energy production.
- Nuts or seeds like chia, flax, or pumpkin seeds for healthy fats and protein that keep you satiated.
- Maca powder or a small amount of matcha for a natural boost without the jitters.

For Immunity: Support your immune system with ingredients rich in antioxidants, vitamins, and minerals. Consider adding:

- Citrus fruits (like oranges, lemons, and limes) for a dose of vitamin C.
- Ginger and turmeric are both anti-inflammatory and known for their immune-supporting properties.
- Berries, which are packed with antioxidants that help combat oxidative stress.

For Detox: Enhance your liver's natural detoxifying functions by including specific ingredients that aid digestion and support liver function:

- Beets and leafy greens, which contain phytonutrients that encourage detoxification.
- Dandelion greens or parsley, both of which have mild diuretic properties to help flush toxins.
- Aloe vera or cucumber hydrating ingredients that support kidney and liver function.

With these tips in mind, you can create balanced, delicious drinks that support liver health and cater to your specific needs—whether it's more energy, immune support, or gentle detoxification. In the following chapters, you'll find a collection of smoothie and mocktail recipes that put these principles into practice. Each recipe is crafted to provide unique benefits for liver support and overall wellness, combining nutrient-dense superfoods, herbs, and hydrating ingredients. Whether you're looking to refresh your day, boost your energy, or nurture your liver with a gentle detox, these drinks are designed to make it easy and enjoyable. Explore, experiment, and feel empowered as you discover a variety of delicious, liver-friendly options to incorporate into your daily routine.

Chapter 3
SMOOTHIE

Cinnamon Pear Smoothie

Yield: 2 servings

Prep Time: 5 minutes

Ingredients :

- 2 ripe pears, cored and chopped
- ½ cup unsweetened almond milk (or any plant-based milk)
- ½ teaspoon ground cinnamon
- 1 tablespoon chia seeds (optional, for extra fiber)
- ½ cup ice cubes
- 1 teaspoon honey or maple syrup (optional)

Procedure :

1. Combine the pears, almond milk, cinnamon, chia seeds (if using), and ice cubes in a blender. Blend until smooth.
2. Taste and adjust sweetness with honey or maple syrup, if desired.
3. Serve immediately, garnishing with a sprinkle of cinnamon.

Nutrition per Serving:

- Calories: 110
- Protein: 2g
- Carbohydrates: 26g
- Fats: 2g
- Fiber: 6g
- Cholesterol: 0mg
- Sodium: 40mg
- Potassium: 200mg

Notes:

- Substitute pears with apples or peaches for a different flavor.
- Use coconut milk instead of almond milk for a creamier, tropical taste.
- If you prefer a richer smoothie, add a tablespoon of nut butter like almond or cashew.

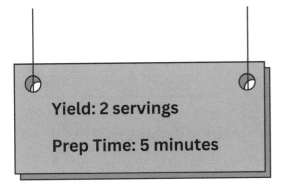
Coconut Mint Green Smoothie

Ingredients :

- 1 cup coconut water
- 1 cup fresh spinach
- ½ avocado
- 1 tablespoon fresh mint leaves
- ½ cup frozen pineapple
- 1 teaspoon chia seeds (optional)
- Ice cubes

Procedure :

1. Combine coconut water, spinach, avocado, mint, frozen pineapple, and chia seeds in a blender.
2. Blend until smooth, adding ice cubes for a chilled texture.
3. Serve immediately in glasses, garnished with mint leaves if desired.

Notes:

- Swap spinach for kale for more fiber and antioxidants.
- Use frozen mango instead of pineapple for a tropical flavor variation.
- Add a tablespoon of hemp seeds for extra protein.

Nutrition per Serving:

- Calories: 140
- Protein: 2g
- Carbohydrates: 20g
- Fats: 7g
- Fiber: 5g
- Cholesterol: 0mg
- Sodium: 60mg
- Potassium: 470mg

Avocado Pineapple Smoothie

Yield: 2 servings

Prep Time: 5 minutes

Ingredients :

- ½ avocado
- 1 cup fresh or frozen pineapple chunks
- 1 cup coconut water
- 1 teaspoon lime juice
- 1 tablespoon chia seeds (optional)
- Ice cubes

Procedure :

1. Blend avocado, pineapple, coconut water, lime juice, and chia seeds until smooth.
2. Pour into glasses and serve immediately, garnished with extra pineapple chunks.

Nutrition per Serving:

- Calories: 160
- Protein: 2g
- Carbohydrates: 25g
- Fats: 7g
- Fiber: 5g
- Cholesterol: 0mg
- Sodium: 60mg
- Potassium: 470mg

Notes:

- Use mango or papaya in place of pineapple for a tropical twist.
- Swap coconut water for almond milk for a creamier texture.
- Add a handful of spinach for a nutritious green boost without affecting the flavor.

Yield: 2 servings

Prep Time: 5 minutes

Orange and Turmeric Glow Smoothie

Ingredients :

- 1 large orange, peeled and segmented
- 1 banana, frozen
- ½ teaspoon ground turmeric
- ½ cup almond milk (or coconut water)
- 1 tablespoon chia seeds (optional)
- ½ cup ice cubes
- A pinch of black pepper (to enhance turmeric absorption)

Procedure :

1. Combine the orange, banana, turmeric, almond milk, chia seeds, and black pepper in a blender.
2. Blend until smooth and creamy. Add ice cubes and blend again for a cold, refreshing smoothie.
3. Serve immediately in glasses, garnished with a sprinkle of turmeric if desired.

Notes:

- Use mango instead of banana for a tropical twist.
- Swap almond milk with coconut water for extra hydration.
- Add a tablespoon of hemp seeds for an extra boost of protein.

Nutrition per Serving:

- Calories: 160
- Protein: 2g
- Carbohydrates: 35g
- Fats: 2g
- Fiber: 5g
- Cholesterol: 0mg
- Sodium: 40mg
- Potassium: 500mg

Green Detox Smoothie

Yield: 2 servings

Prep Time: 5 minutes

Ingredients :

- 1 cup spinach
- ½ cucumber, peeled and chopped
- ½ green apple, cored and sliced
- 1 tablespoon lemon juice
- 1 teaspoon grated ginger
- 1 cup coconut water
- Ice cubes

Procedure :

1. In a blender, combine spinach, cucumber, green apple, lemon juice, ginger, and coconut water.
2. Blend until smooth and creamy. Add ice cubes and blend again for a chilled smoothie.
3. Serve immediately in glasses.

Nutrition per Serving:

- Calories: 50
- Protein: 1g
- Carbohydrates: 12g
- Fats: 0g
- Fiber: 2g
- Cholesterol: 0mg
- Sodium: 60mg
- Potassium: 270mg

Notes:

- Replace spinach with kale for a more robust flavor and extra nutrients.
- Use lime juice instead of lemon for a zestier taste.
- Swap coconut water with unsweetened almond milk for a creamier texture.

Papaya and Lime Smoothie

Ingredients :

- 1 cup ripe papaya, peeled and chopped
- 1 banana
- 1 tablespoon lime juice
- ½ cup coconut milk (unsweetened)
- ½ cup water
- Ice cubes

Procedure :

1. Combine papaya, banana, lime juice, coconut milk, and water in a blender.
2. Blend until smooth and creamy.
3. Serve over ice and enjoy immediately.

Notes:

- Replace banana with mango for a tropical flavor.
- Use almond or soy milk instead of coconut milk for a lighter smoothie.
- Add a pinch of chia seeds for an extra fiber boost and omega-3s.

Nutrition per Serving:

- Calories: 80
- Protein: 1g
- Carbohydrates: 18g
- Fats: 2g
- Fiber: 2g
- Cholesterol: 0mg
- Sodium: 20mg
- Potassium: 230mg

Minted Cucumber and Melon Smoothie

Yield: 2 servings

Prep Time: 5 minutes

Ingredients :

- 1 cup cucumber, peeled and chopped
- 1 cup honeydew melon, chopped
- 1 tablespoon lime juice
- 4-5 fresh mint leaves
- 1 cup coconut water
- Ice cubes

Procedure :

1. Combine cucumber, melon, lime juice, mint leaves, and coconut water in a blender.
2. Blend until smooth and frothy.
3. Serve over ice in glasses, garnished with extra mint leaves.

Nutrition per Serving:

- Calories: 45
- Protein: 1g
- Carbohydrates: 11g
- Fats: 0g
- Fiber: 1g
- Cholesterol: 0mg
- Sodium: 70mg
- Potassium: 170mg

Notes:

- Replace honeydew melon with watermelon or cantaloupe for a different fruity flavor.
- You can use sparkling water instead of coconut water for a refreshing twist.
- Add a teaspoon of honey or agave syrup for extra sweetness if desired.

Kiwi Spinach Green Smoothie

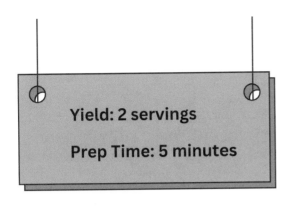

Yield: 2 servings

Prep Time: 5 minutes

Ingredients :

- 2 ripe kiwis, peeled and chopped
- 1 cup fresh spinach
- ½ banana
- ½ cup coconut water
- 1 tablespoon flaxseeds (optional)
- Ice cubes

Procedure :

1. Combine kiwis, spinach, banana, coconut water, and flaxseeds in a blender.
2. Blend until smooth and creamy.
3. Serve over ice, garnished with kiwi slices if desired.

Notes:

- Replace banana with pineapple for a tropical flair.
- Use almond milk instead of coconut water for a creamier texture.
- Add a teaspoon of spirulina powder for an additional nutrient boost.

Nutrition per Serving:

- Calories: 80
- Protein: 2g
- Carbohydrates: 18g
- Fats: 1g
- Fiber: 5g
- Cholesterol: 0mg
- Sodium: 20mg
- Potassium: 300mg

Blueberry Coconut Water Smoothie

Ingredients :

- 1 cup fresh or frozen blueberries
- 1 cup coconut water
- ½ banana
- 1 tablespoon chia seeds (optional)
- Ice cubes

Procedure :

1. Blend blueberries, coconut water, banana, and chia seeds in a blender until smooth.
2. Add ice cubes and blend again for a cool, refreshing drink.
3. Serve immediately.

Nutrition per Serving:

- Calories: 90
- Protein: 1g
- Carbohydrates: 20g
- Fats: 1g
- Fiber: 4g
- Cholesterol: 0mg
- Sodium: 30mg
- Potassium: 150mg

Notes:

- Replace banana with avocado for a creamy texture and additional healthy fats.
- Add a handful of spinach or kale for an extra nutrient boost.
- Swap chia seeds with flaxseeds or hemp seeds for similar health benefits.

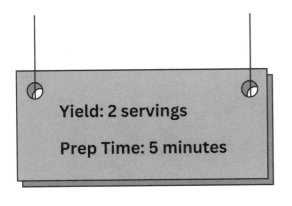

Pea Protein Smoothie with Kiwi and Spinach

Ingredients :

- 1 cup unsweetened almond milk
- 1 kiwi, peeled and sliced
- 1 handful fresh spinach
- 1 scoop pea protein powder
- 1 tablespoon chia seeds
- ½ frozen banana
- Ice cubes (optional)

Procedure :

1. Add almond milk, kiwi, spinach, pea protein powder, chia seeds, and frozen banana to a blender.
2. Blend until smooth, adding ice cubes if desired for a colder texture.
3. Pour into a glass and enjoy immediately.

Notes:

- Use any plant-based milk of choice, like coconut or oat milk.
- Substitute pea protein with your preferred plant-based protein powder.

Nutrition per Serving:

- Calories: 110
- Protein: 7g
- Carbohydrates: 14g
- Fats: 3g
- Fiber: 4g
- Cholesterol: 0mg
- Sodium: 30mg
- Potassium: 300mg

Spirulina Smoothie with Mango and Coconut Water

Yield: 1 servings

Prep Time: 5 minutes

Ingredients :

- 1 cup coconut water
- ½ cup fresh or frozen mango chunks
- 1 teaspoon spirulina powder
- 1 tablespoon ground flaxseed
- ½ cup baby spinach
- ½ frozen banana

Procedure :

1. Combine coconut water, mango, spirulina powder, ground flaxseed, spinach, and frozen banana in a blender.
2. Blend until smooth and creamy.
3. Serve chilled and enjoy.

Nutrition per Serving:

- Calories: 180
- Protein: 3g
- Carbohydrates: 40g
- Fats: 2g
- Fiber: 6g
- Cholesterol: 0mg
- Sodium: 45mg
- Potassium: 520mg

Notes:

- Substitute mango with pineapple for a tropical twist.
- Swap coconut water with filtered water or plant-based milk for a creamier texture.

Turmeric and Ginger Smoothie

Ingredients :

- 1 cup unsweetened almond milk
- ½ teaspoon ground turmeric
- ½ teaspoon grated fresh ginger
- 1 tablespoon honey or maple syrup
- ½ frozen banana
- 1 tablespoon chia seeds
- Pinch of black pepper (to enhance turmeric absorption)
- Ice cubes (optional)

Procedure :

1. In a blender, combine almond milk, turmeric, ginger, honey, frozen banana, chia seeds, and black pepper.
2. Blend until smooth, adding ice if desired.
3. Pour into a glass and serve immediately.

Notes:

- Use cinnamon instead of ginger for a different spice profile.
- Substitute honey with stevia or agave syrup for a lower-glycemic option.

Nutrition per Serving:

- Calories: 150
- Protein: 3g
- Carbohydrates: 25g
- Fats: 4g
- Fiber: 5g
- Cholesterol: 0mg
- Sodium: 50mg
- Potassium: 560mg

Pumpkin Seed and Pear Smoothie

Yield: 2 servings

Prep Time: 5 minutes

Ingredients :

- 1 cup unsweetened oat milk
- 1 ripe pear, cored and chopped
- 2 tablespoons pumpkin seeds
- ½ teaspoon ground cinnamon
- ½ frozen banana
- 1 tablespoon ground flaxseed
- Ice cubes (optional)

Procedure :

1. Place oat milk, pear, pumpkin seeds, cinnamon, frozen banana, and ground flaxseed in a blender.
2. Blend until smooth, adding ice for a colder drink if desired.
3. Serve in a glass and enjoy.

Nutrition per Serving:

- Calories: 110
- Protein: 2g
- Carbohydrates: 17g
- Fats: 4g
- Fiber: 3g
- Cholesterol: 0mg
- Sodium: 12mg
- Potassium: 210mg

Notes:

- Use apple instead of pear for a different flavor.
- Substitute pumpkin seeds with sunflower seeds if preferred.

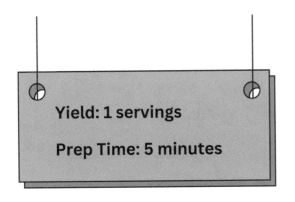

Yield: 1 servings

Prep Time: 5 minutes

Pumpkin Seed and Blueberry Smoothie

Ingredients :

- 1 cup unsweetened coconut milk
- ½ cup fresh or frozen blueberries
- 2 tablespoons pumpkin seeds
- ½ frozen banana
- 1 tablespoon chia seeds
- 1 teaspoon honey or maple syrup (optional)
- Ice cubes (optional)

Procedure :

1. Add coconut milk, blueberries, pumpkin seeds, frozen banana, chia seeds, and honey to a blender.
2. Blend until smooth, adding ice cubes if desired.
3. Pour into a glass and serve chilled.

Notes:

- Use strawberries or blackberries instead of blueberries for variety.
- Replace honey with a few drops of stevia for a sugar-free option.

Nutrition per Serving:

- Calories: 200
- Protein: 5g
- Carbohydrates: 30g
- Fats: 7g
- Fiber: 6g
- Cholesterol: 0mg
- Sodium: 15mg
- Potassium: 490mg

Avocado and Beet Smoothie

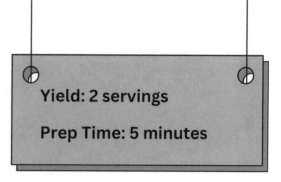

Ingredients :

- ½ medium avocado
- 1 small beet, cooked and peeled
- 1 cup unsweetened almond milk
- ½ cup frozen blueberries
- 1 tablespoon ground flaxseeds
- 1 tablespoon fresh lemon juice
- 1 teaspoon grated ginger (optional, for added anti-inflammatory benefits)
- Ice cubes (optional, for thickness)

Procedure :

1. Place all ingredients in a blender.
2. Blend until smooth and creamy, adding a few ice cubes if you want it colder or thicker.
3. Pour into a glass and enjoy immediately for optimal flavor and freshness.

Nutrition per Serving:

- Calories: 220
- Protein: 3g
- Carbohydrates: 30g
- Fats: 10g
- Fiber: 8g
- Cholesterol: 0mg
- Sodium: 50mg
- Potassium: 620mg

Notes:

- Substitute almond milk with coconut milk or oat milk for a different flavor and creaminess.
- Swap blueberries for strawberries or raspberries if you prefer.
- Replace lemon juice with lime juice for a slightly different citrus kick.

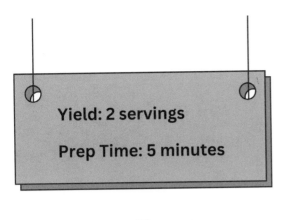

Tropical Detox Smoothie

Ingredients :

- 1 cup pineapple chunks (fresh or frozen)
- ½ cup mango chunks (fresh or frozen)
- 1 small banana
- 1 tablespoon chia seeds
- 1 tablespoon lemon juice
- 1 cup coconut water

Procedure :

1. Blend all ingredients until smooth.
2. Serve immediately, garnished with extra chia seeds if desired.

Notes:

- Use orange juice or almond milk instead of coconut water for a different liquid base.
- Replace banana with avocado for a creamy, lower-sugar version.
- Add a handful of spinach for an extra nutrient boost.

Nutrition per Serving:

- Calories: 160
- Protein: 2g
- Carbohydrates: 35g
- Fats: 2g
- Fiber: 5g
- Cholesterol: 0mg
- Sodium: 50mg
- Potassium: 450mg

Apple, Celery, and Lemon Smoothie

Yield: 1 servings

Prep Time: 5 minutes

Ingredients :

- 1 green apple, cored and chopped
- 1 stalk celery, chopped
- Juice of ½ lemon
- 1 tablespoon chia seeds
- 1 cup cold water
- Ice cubes (optional)

Procedure :

1. Place all ingredients in a blender.
2. Blend until smooth and serve cold.

Nutrition per Serving:

- Calories: 90
- Protein: 1g
- Carbohydrates: 23g
- Fats: 1g
- Fiber: 6g
- Cholesterol: 0mg
- Sodium: 15mg
- Potassium: 300mg

Notes:

- Use cucumber instead of celery for a milder taste.
- Replace water with coconut water for added electrolytes.
- Add a few mint leaves for extra freshness.

Chapter 4

MOCKTAILS

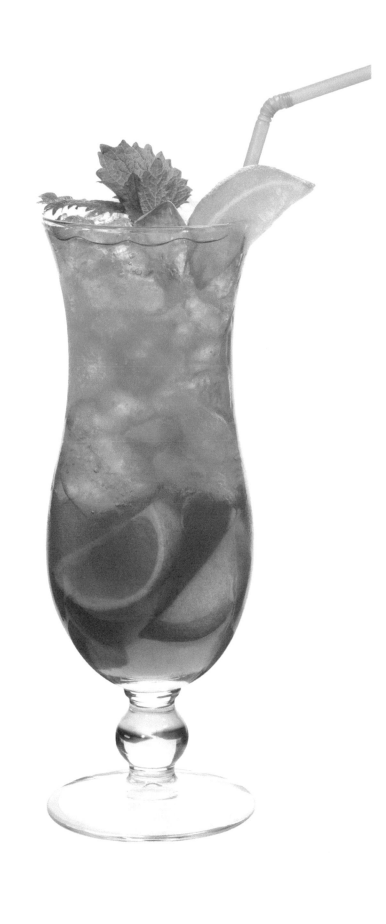

Coconut Water Mojito

Yield: 1 servings

Prep Time: 5 minutes

Ingredients :

- 1 cup coconut water
- ½ cup sparkling water
- 5-6 fresh mint leaves
- 1 tablespoon lime juice
- 1 teaspoon honey or agave syrup (optional)
- Ice cubes

Procedure :

1. Muddle the mint leaves in a glass with lime juice and honey (if using).
2. Pour in the coconut water and sparkling water.
3. Stir and serve over ice cubes, garnished with extra mint leaves.

Nutrition per Serving:

- Calories: 30
- Protein: 0g
- Carbohydrates: 8g
- Fats: 0g
- Fiber: 0g
- Cholesterol: 0mg
- Sodium: 30mg
- Potassium: 200mg

Notes:

- Use lemon juice in place of lime juice for a different citrus twist.
- For a more robust mint flavor, steep the mint in hot water for a few minutes, then let it cool before mixing.
- Replace honey with maple syrup or omit for a lower-sugar version.

Ginger Turmeric Tonic

Ingredients :

- 1-inch piece of fresh ginger, peeled and grated
- 1 teaspoon ground turmeric or 1-inch piece of fresh turmeric, peeled and grated
- 1 tablespoon lemon juice
- 1 tablespoon honey or maple syrup
- 2 cups water
- Ice cubes

Procedure :

1. Blend ginger, turmeric, lemon juice, honey, and water in a blender until well combined.
2. Strain the mixture through a sieve to remove any pulp.
3. Pour over ice cubes and serve immediately.

Notes:

- Use agave syrup or omit the sweetener for a less sugary version.
- Substitute lime juice for lemon juice if you prefer a different citrus flavor.
- Add a pinch of black pepper to help increase the absorption of curcumin from turmeric.

Nutrition per Serving:

- Calories: 40
- Protein: 0g
- Carbohydrates: 10g
- Fats: 0g
- Fiber: 1g
- Cholesterol: 0mg
- Sodium: 10mg
- Potassium: 50mg

Watermelon Basil Refresher

Yield: 2 servings

Prep Time: 5 minutes

Ingredients :

- 2 cups watermelon, chopped
- 5-6 fresh basil leaves
- 1 tablespoon lime juice
- ½ cup water or sparkling water
- Ice cubes

Procedure :

1. Blend watermelon, basil leaves, lime juice, and water until smooth.
2. Strain the mixture through a fine sieve if desired.
3. Serve over ice cubes, garnished with extra basil leaves.

Nutrition per Serving:

- Calories: 30
- Protein: 0g
- Carbohydrates: 8g
- Fats: 0g
- Fiber: 1g
- Cholesterol: 0mg
- Sodium: 5mg
- Potassium: 120mg

Notes:

- Swap lime juice with lemon juice for a different citrus flavor.
- Use mint instead of basil for a refreshing twist.
- Add a splash of coconut water for extra hydration and flavor.

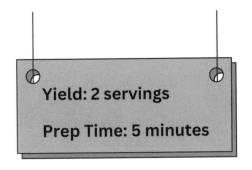

Pineapple Ginger Fizz

Ingredients :

- 1 cup fresh pineapple, chopped
- ½ inch piece of fresh ginger, peeled and grated
- 1 tablespoon lemon juice
- ½ cup sparkling water
- Ice cubes

Procedure :

1. Blend pineapple, ginger, and lemon juice until smooth.
2. Strain the mixture if needed and pour it into a glass.
3. Add sparkling water and ice cubes. Serve immediately.

Notes:

- Use orange juice instead of lemon juice for a sweeter citrus flavor.
- Swap sparkling water with coconut water for a tropical twist.
- Add a pinch of cayenne pepper for a spicy kick.

Nutrition per Serving:

- Calories: 45
- Protein: 1g
- Carbohydrates: 11g
- Fats: 0g
- Fiber: 1g
- Cholesterol: 0mg
- Sodium: 5mg
- Potassium: 100mg

Berry Sparkler

Yield: 2 servings

Prep Time: 5 minutes

Ingredients :

- ½ cup mixed berries (strawberries, blueberries, raspberries, or which you have)
- 1 tablespoon lemon juice
- 1 teaspoon honey (optional)
- 1 cup sparkling water
- Ice cubes

Procedure :

1. Mash the berries in a glass with lemon juice and honey.
2. Add sparkling water and stir well.
3. Serve over ice cubes, garnished with a few whole berries.

Nutrition per Serving:

- Calories: 35
- Protein: 0g
- Carbohydrates: 8g
- Fats: 0g
- Fiber: 1g
- Cholesterol: 0mg
- Sodium: 10mg
- Potassium: 80mg

Notes:

- Use lime juice in place of lemon juice for a tart flavor.
- Replace sparkling water with plain water or coconut water if you prefer a less fizzy drink.
- Swap honey with maple syrup or omit it for a lower-sugar version.

Pear and Ginger Fizz

Ingredients :

- 1 ripe pear, chopped
- 1 teaspoon grated ginger
- 1 tablespoon lemon juice
- 1 cup sparkling water
- Ice cubes

Procedure :

1. Blend the chopped pear, grated ginger, and lemon juice until smooth.
2. Strain the mixture through a fine sieve into a pitcher.
3. Add sparkling water and ice cubes.
4. Serve immediately, garnished with lemon slices if desired.

Notes:

- Use apple instead of pear for a similar flavor profile.
- Swap lemon juice with lime juice for a different citrus twist.
- Add a pinch of cinnamon or nutmeg for extra warmth.

Nutrition per Serving:

- Calories: 50
- Protein: 0g
- Carbohydrates: 13g
- Fats: 0g
- Fiber: 2g
- Cholesterol: 0mg
- Sodium: 10mg
- Potassium: 150mg

Cucumber Mint Cooler

Ingredients :

- 1 cucumber, peeled and chopped
- 1 tablespoon lime juice
- 5-6 fresh mint leaves
- 1 cup sparkling water
- Ice cubes

Procedure :

1. Blend cucumber, lime juice, and mint leaves in a blender until smooth.
2. Strain the mixture through a sieve into a pitcher.
3. Add sparkling water and ice cubes.
4. Serve immediately, garnished with extra mint leaves and cucumber slices.

Nutrition per Serving:

- Calories: 10
- Protein: 0g
- Carbohydrates: 3g
- Fats: 0g
- Fiber: 1g
- Cholesterol: 0mg
- Sodium: 5mg
- Potassium: 100mg

Notes:

- Use lemon juice instead of lime for a different citrus note.
- Add a splash of honey or agave syrup if you prefer a sweeter drink.
- Replace sparkling water with coconut water for a tropical touch.

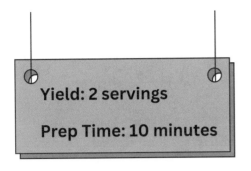
Lavender Lemon Sparkler

Ingredients :

- 1 tablespoon dried culinary lavender
- 1 tablespoon lemon juice
- 1 teaspoon honey or agave syrup (optional)
- 1 cup sparkling water
- Ice cubes
- Lemon slices and fresh lavender sprigs (for garnish)

Procedure :

1. Steep dried lavender in ¼ cup hot water for 5 minutes, then strain to remove the lavender.
2. Mix the lavender tea with lemon juice and honey in a glass.
3. Add sparkling water and ice cubes.
4. Garnish with lemon slices and lavender sprigs before serving.

Notes:

- Use lime juice instead of lemon for a different citrus profile.
- Replace sparkling water with club soda for a lighter fizz.
- Add a splash of elderflower syrup for a floral twist.

Nutrition per Serving:

- Calories: 15
- Protein: 0g
- Carbohydrates: 4g
- Fats: 0g
- Fiber: 0g
- Cholesterol: 0mg
- Sodium: 5mg
- Potassium: 15mg

Cranberry Pomegranate Spritzer

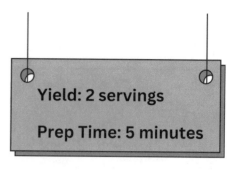

Yield: 2 servings

Prep Time: 5 minutes

Ingredients :

- ½ cup cranberry juice (unsweetened)
- ½ cup pomegranate juice (unsweetened)
- 1 cup sparkling water
- 1 teaspoon lemon juice
- Ice cubes
- Fresh mint leaves (for garnish)

Procedure :

1. Mix cranberry, pomegranate, and lemon juice in a large glass or pitcher.
2. Add sparkling water and stir gently.
3. Serve over ice and garnish with fresh mint leaves.

Nutrition per Serving:

- Calories: 60
- Protein: 0g
- Carbohydrates: 15g
- Fats: 0g
- Fiber: 0g
- Cholesterol: 0mg
- Sodium: 5mg
- Potassium: 110mg

Notes:

- Use orange juice instead of lemon juice for a citrus twist.
- Swap sparkling water for club soda for a lighter fizz.
- Add a teaspoon of agave syrup if you prefer a sweeter taste.

Yield: 2 servings

Prep Time: 10 minutes

Ingredients :

- ½ cucumber, peeled and chopped
- ½ cup aloe vera juice (unsweetened)
- 1 tablespoon lime juice
- 1 teaspoon honey or agave syrup (optional)
- 1 cup water or sparkling water
- Ice cubes
- Fresh mint leaves (for garnish)

Procedure :

1. Blend cucumber, aloe vera juice, lime juice, and honey until smooth.
2. Strain the mixture if desired for a smoother drink.
3. Pour over ice in glasses and garnish with fresh mint leaves.

Notes:

- Swap aloe vera juice with coconut water for extra hydration.
- Add a pinch of sea salt for an electrolyte boost.
- Use lemon juice instead of lime for a more tangy flavor.

Nutrition per Serving:

- Calories: 25
- Protein: 0g
- Carbohydrates: 6g
- Fats: 0g
- Fiber: 0g
- Cholesterol: 0mg
- Sodium: 10mg
- Potassium: 50mg

Apple Cider Vinegar Tonic

Yield: 2 servings

Prep Time: 5 minutes

Ingredients :

- 2 tablespoons apple cider vinegar
- 1 tablespoon honey or agave syrup
- 2 cups cold water
- 1 tablespoon lemon juice
- Ice cubes
- Lemon slices (for garnish)

Procedure :

1. Mix apple cider vinegar, honey, lemon juice, and water in a small pitcher.
2. Pour the tonic over ice in two glasses.
3. Garnish with lemon slices and serve chilled.

Nutrition per Serving:

- Calories: 35
- Protein: 0g
- Carbohydrates: 9g
- Fats: 0g
- Fiber: 0g
- Cholesterol: 0mg
- Sodium: 5mg
- Potassium: 70mg

Notes:

- Add a pinch of cayenne pepper for a metabolism boost.
- Swap honey with maple syrup if preferred.
- Replace half of the water with sparkling water for a fizzy version.

Lemon Ginger Spritzer

Yield: 2 servings

Prep Time: 5 minutes

Ingredients :

- 1 lemon, juiced
- 1 teaspoon fresh ginger, grated
- 1 cup sparkling water
- 1 teaspoon honey or agave syrup (optional)
- Ice cubes
- Lemon slices and mint leaves (for garnish)

Procedure :

1. Juice the lemon and grate the ginger.
2. Mix the lemon juice, ginger, and honey or agave syrup in a small glass or pitcher.
3. Fill two glasses with ice and pour the lemon-ginger mixture equally into each.
4. Top with sparkling water, stir and garnish with lemon slices and mint.

Notes:

- Use lime instead of lemon for a tangier version.
- Let the ginger steep in hot water for a few minutes before mixing for a more intense ginger flavor.
- Add a splash of apple cider vinegar for added liver-friendly benefits.

Nutrition per Serving:

- Calories: 30
- Protein: 0g
- Carbohydrates: 8g
- Fats: 0g
- Fiber: 0g
- Cholesterol: 0mg
- Sodium: 10mg
- Potassium: 60mg

Berry Kombucha Mocktail

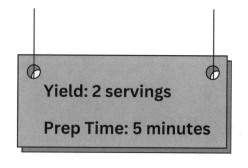

Ingredients :

- 1 cup mixed berries (fresh or frozen)
- 1 cup kombucha (any flavor)
- 1 tablespoon lemon juice
- Ice cubes
- Fresh mint for garnish

Procedure :

1. Muddle the berries at the bottom of a glass.
2. Add kombucha and lemon juice, then stir gently.
3. Serve over ice and garnish with fresh mint.

Nutrition per Serving:

- Calories: 50
- Protein: 0g
- Carbohydrates: 13g
- Fats: 0g
- Fiber: 2g
- Cholesterol: 0mg
- Sodium: 10mg
- Potassium: 150mg

Notes:

- Use sparkling water or coconut water instead of kombucha for a lighter drink.
- Mix kombucha with half water or juice if it is too strong for your taste.
- Replace berries with sliced citrus for a different flavor profile.

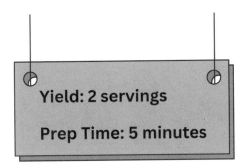
Green Apple and Celery Spritzer

Ingredients :

- 1 green apple, chopped
- 2 celery stalks, chopped
- 1 tablespoon lemon juice
- 1 teaspoon honey (optional)
- 1 cup sparkling water
- Ice cubes

Procedure :

1. Blend the green apple, celery, and lemon juice until smooth.
2. Strain the mixture if you prefer a smoother drink.
3. Mix the juice with sparkling water and serve over ice cubes.

Notes:

- Replace celery with cucumber for a milder flavor.
- Use lime juice instead of lemon juice for a more tart option.
- Skip the honey if you prefer a naturally tart drink, or use stevia for a low-calorie sweetener.

Nutrition per Serving:

- Calories: 50
- Protein: 1g
- Carbohydrates: 13g
- Fats: 0g
- Fiber: 3g
- Cholesterol: 0mg
- Sodium: 30mg
- Potassium: 180mg

Grapefruit and Rosemary Fizz

Yield: 2 servings

Prep Time: 5 minutes

Ingredients :

- 1 large grapefruit, juiced (about 1 cup)
- 1 cup sparkling water
- 1-2 sprigs fresh rosemary
- 1 tablespoon honey or agave syrup (optional)
- Ice cubes
- Grapefruit slices and rosemary sprigs (for garnish)

Procedure :

1. Juice the grapefruit and strain if necessary to remove the pulp.
2. In a shaker or small pitcher, combine the grapefruit juice, honey or agave syrup (if using), and ice. Shake or stir well.
3. Pour the grapefruit mixture evenly into two glasses filled with ice.
4. Top with sparkling water and stir gently. Garnish with grapefruit slices and a sprig of rosemary.

Nutrition per Serving:

- Calories: 70
- Protein: 0g
- Carbohydrates: 18g
- Fats: 0g
- Fiber: 1g
- Cholesterol: 0mg
- Sodium: 20mg
- Potassium: 250mg

Notes:

- Replace grapefruit juice with lemon or lime juice for a different citrus flavor.
- If you're out of sparkling water, use club soda or plain water for a still version.
- For a sweeter taste, increase the honey or agave syrup to your liking.

Chapter 5

OTHER REFRESHING DRINKS

Honeydew Mint Iced Tea

Yield: 2 servings

Prep Time: 5 minutes

Cooking Time: 5 minutes

Ingredients :

- 1 green tea bag
- 1 cup honeydew melon, cubed
- 1 cup cold water
- Fresh mint leaves
- Ice cubes

Procedure :

1. Brew green tea with 1 cup of hot water, then let cool.
2. Blend honeydew melon with cold water until smooth, then strain if desired.
3. Mix green tea and honeydew juice, and pour over ice with mint leaves.

Nutrition per Serving:

- Calories: 20
- Protein: 0g
- Carbohydrates: 5g
- Fats: 0g
- Fiber: 0g
- Cholesterol: 0mg
- Sodium: 5mg
- Potassium: 60mg

Notes:

- Replace honeydew with cantaloupe or watermelon.
- Use cucumber instead of melon for a lighter, less sweet taste.

Strawberry Basil Lemonade

Yield: 2 servings

Prep Time: 5 minutes

Ingredients :

- ½ cup fresh strawberries, hulled and chopped
- 1 tablespoon lemon juice
- 1 teaspoon honey or agave syrup (optional)
- 2-3 fresh basil leaves
- 1 cup water
- Ice cubes
- Lemon slices (for garnish)

Procedure :

1. Blend strawberries, lemon juice, and honey until smooth.
2. Muddle basil leaves at the bottom of the glass, then pour in the strawberry mixture.
3. Add water and ice cubes, stir, and garnish with lemon slices.

Notes:

- Replace strawberries with raspberries for a slightly tangier flavor.
- Use mint leaves instead of basil for a refreshing twist.
- Add a splash of sparkling water for a bubbly version.

Nutrition per Serving:

- Calories: 30
- Protein: 0g
- Carbohydrates: 7g
- Fats: 0g
- Fiber: 1g
- Cholesterol: 0mg
- Sodium: 5mg
- Potassium: 90mg

Lavender Lemonade

Yield: 2 servings

Prep Time: 5 minutes

Cooking Time: 5 minutes

Ingredients :

- 2 cups water
- 1 tablespoon dried lavender flowers
- Juice of 1 lemon
- 1–2 teaspoons honey or maple syrup (optional)
- Ice cubes

Procedure :

1. Bring 1 cup of water to a simmer, add dried lavender, and let steep for 5 minutes.
2. Strain the lavender tea into a pitcher and let it cool.
3. Add lemon juice, remaining water, and sweetener if desired.
4. Serve over ice and enjoy chilled.

Nutrition per Serving:

- Calories: 15
- Protein: 0g
- Carbohydrates: 4g
- Fats: 0g
- Fiber: 0g
- Cholesterol: 0mg
- Sodium: 0mg
- Potassium: 20mg

Notes:

- Use fresh lavender for a more aromatic flavor.
- Replace lemon juice with lime juice for a twist.

Cucumber Melon Slush

Yield: 2 servings

Prep Time: 5 minutes

Ingredients :

- 1 cup cucumber, peeled and diced
- 1 cup honeydew melon, cubed
- 1 tablespoon lime juice
- 1 teaspoon honey or agave syrup (optional)
- 1 cup ice cubes
- Fresh mint leaves (for garnish)

Procedure :

1. Blend the cucumber, honeydew melon, lime juice, honey, and ice cubes in a blender until smooth.
2. Pour into glasses and garnish with fresh mint leaves.
3. Serve chilled for a refreshing slush.

Nutrition per Serving:

- Calories: 45
- Protein: 1g
- Carbohydrates: 11g
- Fats: 0g
- Fiber: 1g
- Cholesterol: 0mg
- Sodium: 5mg
- Potassium: 180mg

Notes:

- Use watermelon instead of honeydew for a sweeter variation.
- Add a tablespoon of chia seeds for added fiber and texture.
- Replace the lime juice with lemon juice for a slightly different citrus flavor.

51

Beet and Berry Detox Juice

Yield: 1 serving

Prep Time: 5 minutes

Cooking Time: 3 minutes

Ingredients :

- 1 small beet, peeled and chopped
- ½ cup mixed berries (blueberries, raspberries, strawberries)
- 1 small apple, cored and sliced
- 1 tablespoon lemon juice
- 1 cup water or coconut water
- Ice cubes

Procedure :

1. Blend beet, berries, apple, lemon juice, and water until smooth.
2. Strain through a fine mesh sieve or cheesecloth for a smoother texture, if desired.
3. Serve over ice and enjoy immediately.

Nutrition per Serving:

- Calories: 90
- Protein: 1g
- Carbohydrates: 22g
- Fats: 0g
- Fiber: 3g
- Cholesterol: 0mg
- Sodium: 15mg
- Potassium: 270mg

Notes:

- Use carrots instead of beet for a milder flavor.
- Add a small piece of ginger for an extra detoxifying boost.
- Swap coconut water with green tea for added antioxidants.

Chia Water with Lemon and Honey

Ingredients :

- 2 cups water
- 1 tablespoon chia seeds
- 1 tablespoon lemon juice
- 1 teaspoon honey or agave syrup (optional)
- Ice cubes
- Lemon slices (for garnish)

Procedure :

1. Mix chia seeds, lemon juice, and honey in water and let it sit for 5 minutes for the chia seeds to expand.
2. Stir occasionally to prevent clumping.
3. Pour over ice in two glasses and garnish with lemon slices.

Notes:

- Add a splash of orange juice for a sweeter citrus flavor.
- Use lime juice instead of lemon for a tangier taste.
- Swap honey with maple syrup or stevia for a different sweetness level.

Nutrition per Serving:

- Calories: 40
- Protein: 1g
- Carbohydrates: 9g
- Fats: 1g
- Fiber: 3g
- Cholesterol: 0mg
- Sodium: 10mg
- Potassium: 30mg

Blueberry Coconut Water Cooler

Yield: 2 serving

Prep Time: 5 minutes

Ingredients :

- 1 cup coconut water
- ½ cup fresh or frozen blueberries
- 1 tablespoon lime juice
- 1 teaspoon honey or agave syrup (optional)
- Ice cubes
- Blueberries and lime slices (for garnish)

Procedure :

1. Blend coconut water, blueberries, lime juice, and honey until smooth.
2. Pour over ice in two glasses and stir.
3. Garnish with extra blueberries and lime slices.

Nutrition per Serving:

- Calories: 60
- Protein: 0g
- Carbohydrates: 15g
- Fats: 0g
- Fiber: 2g
- Cholesterol: 0mg
- Sodium: 40mg
- Potassium: 200mg

Notes:

- Swap blueberries with raspberries or blackberries for a different flavor.
- Use sparkling water instead of coconut water for a lighter, fizzy drink.
- Add a handful of fresh mint leaves for extra freshness.

Mango and Ginger Iced Tea

Yield: 2 servings

Prep Time: 10 minutes

Cooking Time: 10 minutes

Ingredients :

- 2 cups brewed green tea, chilled
- ½ cup fresh mango, diced
- 1 teaspoon fresh ginger, grated
- 1 tablespoon honey or agave syrup (optional)
- Ice cubes
- Mango slices and mint leaves (for garnish)

Procedure :

1. Brew green tea and let it cool.
2. In a blender, blend the mango and ginger with the green tea until smooth.
3. Pour over ice in two glasses.
4. Garnish with mango slices and mint leaves.

Nutrition per Serving:

- Calories: 40
- Protein: 0g
- Carbohydrates: 10g
- Fats: 0g
- Fiber: 1g
- Cholesterol: 0mg
- Sodium: 5mg
- Potassium: 110mg

Notes:

- Use black tea for a more robust flavor.
- Add a splash of lime juice for a citrusy tang.
- Swap mango with peach or pineapple for a tropical twist.

Coconut Lime Chia Fresca

Yield: 2 serving

Prep Time: 10 minutes

Ingredients :

- 2 cups coconut water
- 1 tablespoon chia seeds
- 1 tablespoon lime juice
- 1 teaspoon honey or agave syrup (optional)
- Ice cubes
- Lime wedges (for garnish)

Procedure :

1. Mix coconut water, chia seeds, lime juice, and honey in a small pitcher.
2. Let sit for 5 minutes to allow the chia seeds to expand.
3. Pour over ice in two glasses and garnish with lime wedges.

Nutrition per Serving:

- Calories: 70
- Protein: 1g
- Carbohydrates: 15g
- Fats: 1g
- Fiber: 2g
- Cholesterol: 0mg
- Sodium: 40mg
- Potassium: 300mg

Notes:

- Add a handful of fresh mint for added freshness.
- Use lemon juice instead of lime juice for a different citrus flavor.
- Swap coconut water with plain water for a lighter version.

Mango Mint Lassi

Ingredients :

- 1 cup ripe mango, chopped
- ½ cup plain Greek yogurt
- ½ cup coconut milk
- 5-6 fresh mint leaves
- 1 tablespoon honey (optional)
- Ice cubes

Procedure :

1. Blend mango, Greek yogurt, coconut milk, mint leaves, and honey in a blender until smooth.
2. Add ice cubes and blend again until frothy.
3. Serve immediately, garnished with extra mint leaves if desired.

Notes:

- Use almond milk or dairy yogurt if preferred, adjusting for creaminess.
- Swap honey with maple syrup or omit for a naturally sweet option.
- Add a pinch of cardamom for a fragrant, traditional touch.

Nutrition per Serving:

- Calories: 120
- Protein: 4g
- Carbohydrates: 18g
- Fats: 5g
- Fiber: 2g
- Cholesterol: 5mg
- Sodium: 30mg
- Potassium: 200mg

Kiwi Cucumber Refresher

Yield: 2 serving

Prep Time: 5 minutes

Ingredients :

- 2 kiwis, peeled and chopped
- ½ cucumber, chopped
- 1 tablespoon fresh mint leaves
- 1 cup cold water
- 1 teaspoon honey or agave syrup (optional)
- Ice cubes
- Kiwi slices (for garnish)

Procedure :

1. Blend the kiwis, cucumber, mint, and cold water until smooth.
2. Strain through a sieve if you prefer a smoother drink.
3. Pour over ice, and garnish with kiwi slices and extra mint leaves.

Nutrition per Serving:

- Calories: 50
- Protein: 1g
- Carbohydrates: 13g
- Fats: 0g
- Fiber: 3g
- Cholesterol: 0mg
- Sodium: 10mg
- Potassium: 250mg

Notes:

- Swap kiwi with green apple or pineapple for a different refreshing twist.
- Use coconut water instead of regular water for added hydration.
- Add a tablespoon of lime juice for a citrusy kick.

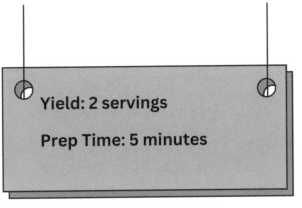

Papaya Coconut Lassi

Ingredients :

- 1 cup ripe papaya, cubed
- ½ cup unsweetened coconut yogurt (or regular plain yogurt)
- ½ cup coconut milk (light or full-fat)
- 1 tablespoon lime juice
- 1 teaspoon honey or agave syrup (optional)
- Ice cubes
- Lime wedges (for garnish)

Procedure :

1. Blend the papaya, coconut yogurt, coconut milk, lime juice, and honey until smooth.
2. Add ice cubes and blend again until well-chilled.
3. Serve in glasses, garnished with lime wedges.

Notes:

- Replace papaya with mango or pineapple for a tropical twist.
- Use almond yogurt if you prefer a non-coconut version.
- Add a pinch of turmeric for an extra anti-inflammatory boost.

Nutrition per Serving:

- Calories: 140
- Protein: 2g
- Carbohydrates: 20g
- Fats: 6g
- Fiber: 2g
- Cholesterol: 0mg
- Sodium: 25mg
- Potassium: 270mg

Orange and Carrot Sunrise

Yield: 2 serving

Prep Time: 5 minutes

Ingredients :

- 2 large oranges, juiced (about 1 cup)
- 1 large carrot, peeled and juiced (or finely grated and squeezed)
- ½ teaspoon grated ginger (optional)
- ½ cup cold water or coconut water
- Ice cubes
- Orange slices (for garnish)

Procedure :

1. Juice the oranges and carrots. If you don't have a juicer, finely grate the carrot and squeeze the juice through a cheesecloth or fine sieve.
2. Combine the orange juice, carrot juice, and cold water in a glass or pitcher. Stir well.
3. Add grated ginger for a spicy kick (optional).
4. Serve over ice and garnish with orange slices.

Nutrition per Serving:

- Calories: 80
- Protein: 1g
- Carbohydrates: 20g
- Fats: 0g
- Fiber: 2g
- Cholesterol: 0mg
- Sodium: 40mg
- Potassium: 300mg

Notes:

- If you don't have fresh carrots, substitute them with store-bought carrot juice or skip it for a simple orange drink.
- Add a splash of lemon juice for extra tanginess.
- Replace water with coconut water for added hydration and flavor.

Citrus Cooler

Ingredients :

- 1 orange, juiced
- 1 lemon, juiced
- 1 lime, juiced
- 1 tablespoon honey or agave syrup
- 1 ½ cups cold water
- Ice cubes
- Fresh mint leaves (optional)

Procedure :

1. Mix the fresh orange, lemon, and lime juices in a large glass.
2. Add honey or agave syrup and stir until fully dissolved.
3. Pour in the cold water and stir to combine.
4. Serve over ice cubes and garnish with mint leaves, if desired.

Notes:

- Substitute grapefruit juice for orange juice for a tangier flavor.
- For a lower-sugar option, omit honey or use a sugar-free sweetener.
- You can also swap the cold water with sparkling water for added fizz.

Nutrition per Serving:

- Calories: 45
- Protein: 1g
- Carbohydrates: 12g
- Fats: 0g
- Fiber: 1g
- Cholesterol: 0mg
- Sodium: 5mg
- Potassium: 160mg

CHAPTER 6
WARM BEVERAGES

Matcha Ginger Warm-Up

Yield: 2 servings

Prep Time: 5 minutes

Cooking Time: 5 minutes

Ingredients :

- 2 cups almond milk (or milk of choice)
- 1 teaspoon matcha green tea powder
- 1 teaspoon grated ginger
- 1–2 teaspoons honey or maple syrup (optional)

Procedure :

1. Warm almond milk in a saucepan over medium heat, but do not let it boil.
2. Whisk in matcha powder and grated ginger until smooth and combined, about 3–4 minutes.
3. Remove from heat and add honey or maple syrup if desired. Pour into mugs and enjoy warm.

Notes:

- For a smoother texture, strain the drink before pouring into mugs.
- Replace almond milk with coconut milk for a richer consistency.

Nutrition per Serving:

- Calories: 45
- Protein: 1g
- Carbohydrates: 8g
- Fats: 2g
- Fiber: 1g
- Cholesterol: 0mg
- Sodium: 30mg
- Potassium: 50mg

Spiced Apple Cider

Yield: 4 servings

Prep Time: 5 minutes

Cooking Time: 10 minutes

Ingredients :

- 4 cups apple cider (unsweetened)
- 1 cinnamon stick
- 4 whole cloves
- ½ teaspoon ground nutmeg
- 1 tablespoon lemon juice
- 1 teaspoon honey or maple syrup (optional)
- Apple slices and cinnamon sticks (for garnish)

Procedure :

1. Heat apple cider, cinnamon stick, cloves, nutmeg, and lemon juice in a saucepan over medium heat.
2. Simmer for 10 minutes, stirring occasionally.
3. Strain the cider to remove the spices.
4. Serve warm with apple slices and an extra cinnamon stick for garnish.

Notes:

- Use pear juice instead of apple cider for a different flavor profile.
- Swap honey with maple syrup for a more profound sweetness.
- Add a dash of ground ginger for a spicier kick.

Nutrition per Serving:

- Calories: 90
- Protein: 0g
- Carbohydrates: 24g
- Fats: 0g
- Fiber: 1g
- Cholesterol: 0mg
- Sodium: 5mg
- Potassium: 200mg

Peppermint Hot Cocoa

Ingredients :

- 2 cups unsweetened almond milk (or milk of choice)
- 2 tablespoons unsweetened cocoa powder
- 1 tablespoon maple syrup
- ¼ teaspoon peppermint extract
- Dark chocolate shavings (for garnish, optional)

Procedure :

1. Heat almond milk in a small saucepan over medium heat until warm but not boiling.
2. Whisk in cocoa powder and maple syrup until smooth and heated through, about 3–4 minutes.
3. Remove from heat, stir in peppermint extract, and pour into mugs.
4. Garnish with dark chocolate shavings if desired.

Notes:

- Swap peppermint extract with a dash of cinnamon for a different flavor.
- Use oat milk for a creamy texture.

Nutrition per Serving:

- Calories: 70
- Protein: 2g
- Carbohydrates: 11g
- Fats: 2g
- Fiber: 2g
- Cholesterol: 0mg
- Sodium: 60mg
- Potassium: 180mg

Golden Turmeric Latte

Yield: 2 servings

Prep Time: 5 minutes

Cooking Time: 5 minutes

Ingredients :

- 2 cups unsweetened almond milk (or milk of choice)
- 1 teaspoon ground turmeric
- ½ teaspoon ground cinnamon
- ½ teaspoon grated ginger (or ¼ teaspoon ground ginger)
- 1 teaspoon honey or maple syrup (optional)
- A pinch of black pepper (to enhance turmeric absorption)

Procedure :

1. In a small saucepan, heat the almond milk over medium heat until warm but not boiling.
2. Add the turmeric, cinnamon, ginger, and black pepper, stirring well to combine.
3. Continue to stir until the mixture is warmed through and spices are dissolved, about 3–5 minutes.
4. Remove from heat, stir in honey or maple syrup if desired, and pour into mugs.

Nutrition per Serving:

- Calories: 40
- Protein: 1g
- Carbohydrates: 8g
- Fats: 2g
- Fiber: 1g
- Cholesterol: 0mg
- Sodium: 60mg
- Potassium: 110mg

Notes:

- Swap almond milk for coconut milk for a richer flavor.
- Add a dash of vanilla extract for a sweeter aroma.

Hot Apple Cinnamon Oat Smoothie

Yield: 2 servings

Prep Time: 5 minutes

Cooking Time: 5 minutes

Ingredients :

- 1 cup unsweetened apple juice
- 1 cup oat milk (or milk of choice)
- ½ teaspoon ground cinnamon
- 2 tablespoons rolled oats
- 1 teaspoon honey or maple syrup (optional)

Procedure :

1. Combine apple juice, oat milk, cinnamon, and oats in a blender. Blend until smooth.
2. Pour mixture into a saucepan and heat over medium-low, stirring until warm, about 5 minutes.
3. Pour into mugs, adding honey or maple syrup if desired.

Notes:

- Use almond milk instead of oat milk for a lighter version.
- Add a dash of nutmeg or ginger for extra spice.

Nutrition per Serving:

- Calories: 80
- Protein: 1g
- Carbohydrates: 15g
- Fats: 2g
- Fiber: 2g
- Cholesterol: 0mg
- Sodium: 20mg
- Potassium: 120mg

Coconut Matcha Latte

Yield: 1 serving

Prep Time: 5 minutes

Cooking Time: 3 minutes

Ingredients :

- 1 teaspoon matcha powder
- 1 cup coconut milk (unsweetened)
- 1 teaspoon honey or maple syrup (optional)
- ¼ teaspoon vanilla extract
- Hot water (about 2 tablespoons)

Procedure :

1. Whisk the matcha powder with hot water in a small bowl until it becomes a smooth paste.
2. Heat the coconut milk in a small saucepan over medium heat until warm (but not boiling).
3. Stir in honey and vanilla extract.
4. Pour the coconut milk over the matcha paste and whisk until frothy.
5. Serve immediately.

Nutrition per Serving:

- Calories: 120
- Protein: 1g
- Carbohydrates: 4g
- Fats: 12g
- Fiber: 0g
- Cholesterol: 0mg
- Sodium: 40mg
- Potassium: 150mg

Notes:

- You can use oat milk instead of coconut milk for a different texture and flavor.
- Swap honey for agave syrup or stevia for a low-calorie sweetener option.
- Add a pinch of cinnamon for extra warmth and flavor.

Vanilla Chai Oat Milk Latte

Yield: 2 servings

Prep Time: 5 minutes

Cooking Time: 10 minutes

Ingredients :

- 2 cups oat milk (or milk of choice)
- 1 black tea bag
- ½ teaspoon ground cinnamon
- ¼ teaspoon ground ginger
- ¼ teaspoon ground cardamom
- 1 teaspoon vanilla extract
- 1–2 teaspoons honey or maple syrup (optional)

Procedure :

1. Heat oat milk in a saucepan over medium heat. Add the tea bag, cinnamon, ginger, and cardamom, stirring gently.
2. Let the mixture simmer for 5–7 minutes to blend the spices.
3. Remove from heat, discard the tea bag, and add vanilla extract and honey or maple syrup if desired. Pour into mugs.

Notes:

- Swap oat milk with almond or coconut milk for a lighter or creamier texture.
- Add a pinch of ground cloves or black pepper for an extra spice kick.

Nutrition per Serving:

- Calories: 60
- Protein: 1g
- Carbohydrates: 10g
- Fats: 2g
- Fiber: 1g
- Cholesterol: 0mg
- Sodium: 60mg
- Potassium: 80mg

Creamy Almond Chai

Yield: 2 servings

Prep Time: 5 minutes

Cooking Time: 10 minutes

Ingredients :

- 2 cups almond milk (or milk of choice)
- 1 black tea bag
- ½ teaspoon ground cinnamon
- ¼ teaspoon ground cardamom
- ¼ teaspoon ground ginger
- 1–2 teaspoons maple syrup or honey (optional)

Procedure :

1. Heat almond milk in a saucepan over medium heat. Add the black tea bag, cinnamon, cardamom, and ginger.
2. Let the mixture gently simmer for 5–7 minutes, stirring occasionally.
3. Remove from heat, discard the tea bag, and stir in maple syrup or honey if desired. Pour into mugs.

Nutrition per Serving:

- Calories: 40
- Protein: 1g
- Carbohydrates: 6g
- Fats: 2g
- Fiber: 0g
- Cholesterol: 0mg
- Sodium: 40mg
- Potassium: 60mg

Notes:

- Use coconut milk for a creamier texture.
- Add a pinch of black pepper for a traditional chai spice kick.

Cinnamon Coconut Hot Chocolate

Ingredients :

- 2 cups coconut milk (or milk of choice)
- 2 tablespoons unsweetened cocoa powder
- 1 teaspoon cinnamon
- 1 teaspoon honey or maple syrup (optional)

Procedure :

1. In a saucepan, heat coconut milk over medium heat. Add cocoa powder and cinnamon, stirring until smooth.
2. Remove from heat, add honey or maple syrup if desired, and pour into mugs.

Notes:

- Use almond milk instead of coconut milk for a lighter drink.
- Add a dash of vanilla extract for added flavor.

Nutrition per Serving:

- Calories: 90
- Protein: 1g
- Carbohydrates: 8g
- Fats: 6g
- Fiber: 2g
- Cholesterol: 0mg
- Sodium: 20mg
- Potassium: 150mg

Warm Orange Cinnamon Spice

Yield: 2 servings

Prep Time: 5 minutes

Cooking Time: 10 minutes

Ingredients :

- 2 cups fresh orange juice
- 1 cinnamon stick
- 2 whole cloves
- 1 star anise (optional)
- 1 teaspoon honey or maple syrup (optional)

Procedure :

1. In a saucepan, heat orange juice, cinnamon stick, cloves, and star anise over medium-low heat.
2. Let the mixture gently simmer for 5–7 minutes, allowing spices to infuse.
3. Remove from heat, strain, and pour into mugs. Sweeten with honey or maple syrup if desired.

Nutrition per Serving:

- Calories: 80
- Protein: 1g
- Carbohydrates: 18g
- Fats: 0g
- Fiber: 1g
- Cholesterol: 0mg
- Sodium: 0mg
- Potassium: 250mg

Notes:

- For a tangy twist, add a splash of cranberry juice.
- Use a pinch of ground cinnamon if whole cinnamon sticks aren't available.

Cinnamon Vanilla Rice Milk Delight

Yield: 2 servings

Prep Time: 5 minutes

Cooking Time: 5 minutes

Ingredients :

- 2 cups rice milk (or milk of choice)
- ½ teaspoon ground cinnamon
- ½ teaspoon vanilla extract
- 1 teaspoon honey or maple syrup (optional)

Procedure :

1. Heat rice milk in a saucepan over medium heat until warm.
2. Stir in cinnamon and vanilla extract, mixing until well blended, about 3–4 minutes.
3. Remove from heat and add honey or maple syrup if desired. Pour into mugs and enjoy.

Notes:

- Swap rice milk with oat or almond milk for a different flavor.
- Add a pinch of nutmeg for a warm, cozy touch.

Nutrition per Serving:

- Calories: 70
- Protein: 0g
- Carbohydrates: 15g
- Fats: 1g
- Fiber: 0g
- Cholesterol: 0mg
- Sodium: 20mg
- Potassium: 30mg

Conclusion

Integrating liver-friendly drinks, smoothies, and mocktails into your daily routine is a straightforward yet powerful way to bolster overall health and vitality. Each recipe in this book has been carefully crafted with ingredients that not only taste great but also provide your body with the essential nutrients, antioxidants, and hydration it needs to flourish.

As you've discovered, taking small, intentional steps toward liver health through balanced, nutrient-rich beverages can make a significant difference. From the hydrating benefits of herbs and spices to the nutrient-dense power of superfoods, these recipes are designed to nourish your body while catering to your unique wellness goals—whether it's a gentle detox, immune boost, or energy lift.

Remember, creating a healthy drink routine doesn't have to be complicated. By integrating these recipes into your day, you're adding variety, flavor, and purpose to each sip, supporting not only your liver but your entire body. And don't forget, hydration is one of the most accessible ways to prioritize wellness.

Thank you for taking this journey toward liver care and holistic health. May this collection inspire you to continue making mindful choices for your body, and may each sip bring you closer to vibrant health and wellness.

I extend my best wishes for your well-being.

Made in the USA
Columbia, SC
23 November 2024

47256050R00041